# THE DON'T LAUGH CHALLENGE™

## JOKE BOOK

### HALLOWEEN EDITION

# PRIZES!

# $50 GIFT CARD

## Think YOU can win our JOKE CONTEST?!?!

The Don't Laugh Challenge is having a CONTEST to see who is the MOST HILARIOUS boy or girl in the USA.

Please have your parents email us your best **original** joke and you could win a $50 gift card to Amazon.

Here are the rules:

1. It must be funny. Please do not give us jokes that aren't funny. We get enough of those from our joke writers

2. It must be original. We have computers and we know how to use them.

3. No help from the parents. Plus, they aren't even that funny anyway!!

### Email your best joke to:
 Bacchuspublish@gmail.com

Winners will be announced via email.

Bacchus Publishing House

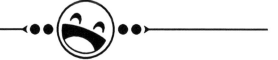

# THE DON'T LAUGH™ CHALLENGE INSTRUCTIONS:

- **SIT DOWN FACING YOUR OPPONENT AT EYE LEVEL.**

- **TAKE TURNS READING JOKES TO EACH OTHER.**

- **FIRST PERSON TO MAKE THE OPPONENT LAUGH, WINS A POINT!**

- **FIRST PERSON TO 3 POINTS WINS & IS CROWNED THE DON'T LAUGH MASTER.**

# HALLOWEEN
## JOKES

WHAT IS A MUMMY'S FAVORITE TYPE OF MUSIC?

RAP.

WHAT IS IT CALLED WHEN A MONSTER SNEEZES?

FRANKEN-SLIME.

WHAT IS A GHOST'S FAVORITE FRUIT?

BOO-BERRIES

WHY ARE THERE NO ZOMBIE POLITICIANS?

THEY CAN'T RUN.

WHY DID THE PUMPKIN LOVE THE CANDLE?

IT MADE IT ALL WARM INSIDE.

WHY WAS THE PUMPKIN WINNING SO MUCH?

IT WAS ON A ROLL.

WHAT ARE ZOMBIES FAVORITE BIRDS?

CRAAAAAAANES

HOW DID THE JACK-O-LANTERN FEEL AFTER IT WAS COMPLIMENTED?

IT WAS GLOWING.

WHY DO WEREWOLVES NOT LIKE CLOUDS?

THEY HAVE A SILVER LINING.

WHY CAN'T APPLES GO
TRICK OR TREATING?

THEY ALWAYS GET SPOILED.

WHY DID NO ONE WANT TO PLAY THE
ZOMBIE SOCCER TEAM?

THEY'RE STIFF COMPETITION.

WHAT IS A WITCHES FAVORITE THING
TO LEARN IN SCHOOL?

SPELLING.

# WHAT DO YOU CALL A BEE THAT LEARNED MAGIC?

BEE WITCHED.

# HOW DID THE WITCHES HAT WIN THE ARGUMENT?

IT MADE A GOOD POINT.

# WHY DID THE WITCHES BROOM HAVE SUCH A BIG EGO?

IT COULDN'T STAY GROUNDED.

# WHY DON'T MUMMIES EAT SANDWICHES?

THEY PREFER WRAPS.

# WHAT PLACE DID THE VAMPIRE COME IN DURING THE RACE?

DEAD LAST.

# HOW DO PUMPKINS ALWAYS STAY SUCH GOOD FRIENDS?

THEY ALWAYS PATCH THINGS UP.

# WHAT DO BANANA PEELS SAY ON HALLOWEEN?

TRIP OR TREAT.

# WHY DIDN'T THE PUMPKIN WANT TO GO TO THE MOVIE?

IT HEARD IT WAS A SMASH HIT.

WHY DIDN'T THE SKELETON CONCERT
GO VERY WELL?

IT WAS A PRETTY THIN CROWD.

WHAT DID THE LIGHTBULB GO
AS FOR HALLOWEEN?

FLASH.

WHY ARE PUMPKINS AFRAID OF
CALENDARS AND HEIGHTS?

THEY NEVER MAKE IT PAST THE FALL.

WHAT PART OF THE JOB
DO SKELETONS HATE?

BREAKS.

WHAT IS THE BEST VEGETABLE
ON HALLOWEEN?

CANDY CORN.

WHAT DID THE KNIFE GO
AS FOR HALLOWEEN?

A DINO-SWORD.

HOW DID THE PUMPKIN FEEL WHEN NO
ONE PICKED HIM FOR THE TEAM?

SQUASHED.

WHAT BASEBALL FOOD IS GOOD
TO EAT ON OCTOBER 31?

HALLOWEENIES.

WHY DID DR. FRANKENSTEIN SEW
HIS MONSTER'S HEAD CLOSED AT
THE LAUNDROMAT?

TO KEEP HIM FROM GETTING BRAINWASHED.


WHERE DO VAMPIRES INVEST THEIR MONEY?

BLOOD BANKS!


HOW DO YOU KNOW WHEN A ZOMBIE WAS THE
LAST TO USE A DECK OF CARDS?

ALL THE HEARTS HAVE BEEN EATEN!


WHY DID THE SCISSORS DRESS AS A
COMPUTER FOR HALLOWEEN?

IT WAS CUTTING-EDGE TECHNOLOGY.

WHY DID THE COACH BRING IN A
JACK-O-LANTERN BEFORE THE BIG GAME?

HE WAS PUMPKIN THEM UP.


WHY WAS THE ZOMBIE SO EMOTIONAL?

HE WAS WEARING HIS HEART ON HIS SLEEVE.


WHY DO GHOSTS NEED BAND-AIDS?

FOR BOO-BOOS.


WHAT IS IT CALLED WHEN DRACULA SLEEPS
IN THE WRONG COFFIN?

A GRAVE MISTAKE

# HOW DID THE ZOMBIE DO HER HAIR?

## BRAAAAAIDS

# WHY DID THE SKELETON FEEL SO SAD?

## HE WAS EMPTY INSIDE.

# HOW DO YOU FIX A BROKEN JACK-O-LANTERN?

## WITH A PUMPKIN PATCH

# WHAT DID THE VEGETARIAN HAND OUT FOR HALLOWEEN?

## CANDY CORN

# WHAT DO YOU CALL A MONSTER THAT LOVES TO PLAY JOKES?

PRANK-ENSTEIN

# WHY DID THE WEREWOLF DRESS UP AS A WIZARD FOR HALLOWEEN?

HE WAS HAIRY POTTER

# WHY DID THE CORN DRESS AS A WEREWOLF FOR HALLOWEEN?

IT WAS A CORN DOG

# WHY DID THE ZOMBIE WITHOUT ANY LIMBS CRAWL AWAY?

HE WAS UNARMED.

# WHAT DID THEY CALL THE QUEEN BEE AFTER SHE BECAME A WITCH?

SPELLING BEE

# WHY DID THE JACK-O-LANTERN TAKE THE OTHER JACK-O-LANTERN TRICK OR TREATING?

IT WAS HIS PUMP-KIN

# WHY DID THE ZOMBIE STRUGGLE IN SCHOOL?

HE HAD NO BRAAAAAINS

# WHY DID NO ONE THINK THE JACK-O-LANTERN WAS SINCERE?

IT PUT ON A FAKE SMILE

# WHAT DO CLOCKS SAY ON HALLOWEEN?

## TICK OR TREAT

# WHO IS THE SMARTEST OF ALL THE MONSTERS?

## FRANK-EINSTEIN

# HOW DID THE ZOMBIE TAKE BREAKING UP WITH HIS GIRLFRIEND?

## HE FELL APART

# WHY WOULDN'T THE SKELETON GO ON STAGE?

## IT WAS WORRIED ABOUT BREAKING A LEG

## WHAT DOES A PUMPKIN SAY IF YOU SCARE IT?

OH MY GOURD

## WHY WAS THE SKELETON STUDYING SO HARD BEFORE THE TEST?

TO BONE UP

## HOW DOES A GHOST SEARCH FOR THINGS ON THE INTERNET?

BOO-GLE

## WHAT DO WITCHES LOVE ABOUT SCHOOL?

SHOW AND SPELL

WHAT DO YOU CALL A MONSTER IN
A BAD MOOD?

CRANK-ENSTEIN

WHAT DO YOU CALL A WOODEN
STICK WITH WINGS?

A BAT

WHAT DO YOU CALL A ZOMBIE
WITH CHILDREN?

MUMMY

HOW WAS THE WIZARD KICKED
OUT OF SCHOOL?

HE WAS CAST OUT

# Why Were the Jack-o-Lanterns Out of Order?

No one orange-d them

# Why Do Ghosts Spend So Long on the Phone?

They get caught up in ghoul talk.

# Why Did the Lonely Monster Move to Egypt?

He had a face only a mummy could love.

# Why Didn't the Zombie Eat the Corpse?

It was a no-brainer

## What do ghosts eat for a quick snack?

Ghoul-nola bars

## Why don't vampires bite zombies?

They have bad blood

## How do you catch a ghost of a bee?

A boo-bee trap

## How do you start a conversation with a yeti?

You break the ice

# How did the werewolf get the promotion?

It's a dog eat dog world.

# How do owls feel about Halloween night?

They don't give a hoot

# Why was the zombie so tired after work?

He had to work the graveyard shift

# How come you never see zombies coming?

They lay low

WHY CAN YOU TRUST A SKELETON
WHILE PLAYING A GAME?

HE HAS NOTHING UP HIS SLEEVES

HOW DOES A MUMMY CALL IT A DAY?

BY WRAPPING THINGS UP

WHAT IS A ZOMBIE'S FAVORITE KIND
OF GET TOGETHER?

A MEAT AND GREET

WHAT IS A PUMPKINS FAVORITE SPORT?

SQUASH

## WHAT IS A GHOST'S FAVORITE SMOOTHIE FLAVOR?

BOO-BERRY.

## WHY DID THE SKELETON NEED TO TAKE A NAP?

BECAUSE HE WAS DEAD TIRED.

## WHERE DO VAMPIRES GO FOR FAST FOOD?

A BLOOD DRIVE.

## WHAT DO YOU CALL A SCARY HORSE?

A NIGHT-MARE.

**WHAT DID THE GHOST SAY TO HIS GIRLFRIEND ON HALLOWEEN?**

"YOU LOOK BOO-TIFUL!"

**WHAT DID IGOR SAY TO DR. FRANKENSTEIN WHEN HE WAS TOLD TO FIND HIM THE RIGHT ORGAN?**

"I DIDN'T KNOW YOU PLAYED THE ORGAN!"

**WHAT DID THE MAGICIAN DO WHEN THE CHILDREN YELLED TRICK OR TREAT AT HIM?**

HE PULLED A RABBIT OUT OF HIS HAT!

**WHAT DO YOU CALL A PILE OF HEAVY BONES?**

A SKELE-TON!

WHAT KIND OF POTATO IS DRACULA
BEST AT PREPARING?

THE MONSTER MASH!

HOW DID THE VAMPIRE DESCRIBE
THE HALLOWEEN PARTY?

"IT WAS FANG-TASTIC!"

HOW DID THE PUMPKIN FEEL AFTER BEING
TURNED INTO A JACK-O-LANTERN?

GUTTED!

WHY DID THE WITCH FAIL WITCH SCHOOL?

BECAUSE SHE DIDN'T KNOW HOW TO SPELL!

# WHY WEREN'T THE DEAD ABLE TO REST IN PEACE?

## TOO MUCH COFFIN!

# HOW DO VAMPIRES PLAY BASEBALL?

## BY USING THEIR BATS!

# WHAT'S A GHOST'S FAVORITE KIND OF FOOD?

## GHOULASH!

# WHAT'S A ZOMBIE'S FAVORITE KIND OF STORM?

## A BRAINSTORM!

# What do you call a dead host?

## A ghost!

# How did the wizard get back at his enemy?

## He yelled a curse!

# What did the witch call her toad?

## Ex-boyfriend!

# How did Frankenstein respond to the joke?

## It had him in stitches!

WHAT INSTRUMENT DOES A SKELETON PLAY?

THE TROMBONE!

WHAT DID THE AX MURDERER SAY WHEN
HIS FRIEND TOLD HIM HE WANTED TO
ASK A GIRL TO THE DANCE?

"I ALREADY AXED HER!"

WHAT DO YOU CALL AN ITEM THAT IS
OWNED BY A GHOST?

SPIRITUALLY POSSESSED!

HOW DID THE LARGE GREEN MAN FEEL
ABOUT FIDGET SPINNERS?

HE WAS SO OGRE IT!

**WHAT DO YOU CALL SOMEONE WHO'S SCARILY GOOD AT DANCING?**

The Boogie-Man!

**WHAT ROUTE DOES A COLD-BLOODED KILLER TAKE TO GET HOME?**

The psychopath!

**WHERE DOES THE SKULL SIT FOR DINNER?**

At the head of the table.

**WHAT'S A WEREWOLF'S LEAST FAVORITE DANCE?**

The moonwalk!

**WHAT DO YOU CALL AN IRRITATED YETTI?**

Furryious!

**HOW DID THE WEREWOLF BECOME THE LEADER OF THE MONSTER GANG?**

He clawed his way to the top!

**WHAT'S DRACULA'S FAVORITE SODA?**

Dra-cola!

**WHAT DO YOU CALL AN UNDEAD BEE?**

A zom-bee!

# What did one Jack'o lantern say to the other?

"I feel empty inside!"

# How do you make a skeleton laugh?

Tickle his funny bone!

# Why did the lights go out when the murderer entered the room?

He killed the lights!

# How did the murderer win the contest?

He slayed the competition!

# What did the arguing skeleton say to the other?

"I have a bone to pick with you!"

# What do you call a witch who likes to play at the beach?

A sandwitch!

# What did the Halloween candle say?

"Does this pumpkin make me look fat?!"

# How did the ghost take his coffee?

One sugar, two screams!

WHAT IS THE GOLDEN RULE OF HALLOWEEN?

TREAT ME THE WAY YOU WANT TO BE TREATED.

WHAT DID ONE GHOST SAY TO THE
OTHER AFTER IT ATE TOO
MUCH HALLOWEEN CANDY?

I'M FEELING SCREAM-ISH.

WHY DO GHOSTS ALWAYS GET
CAUGHT LYING?

EVERYONE CAN SEE RIGHT THROUGH THEM.

WHAT DO YOU CALL A WITCH'S GARAGE?

A BROOM CLOSET!

# What's a Vampire's Favorite Position in Baseball?

## Bat boy!

# What Do You Call the Children in a Jack-o-Lantern Family?

## Pumpkids

# What is a Ghosts Favorite Footwear?

## A boo-t

# How Did the Ghost Make the Cheerleader Team?

## It has a lot of spirit

HOW CAN YOU TELL JACK-O-LANTERNS
LIKE HALLOWEEN?

THEY REALLY LIGHT UP

HOW DID THE SPIDER ORDER
HALLOWEEN DECORATIONS?

HE GOT ON THE WEB

WHAT DOES THE SHOE SAY
ON HALLOWEEN?

TRICK OR FEET

WHAT DOES A PIRATE USE TO
CALL HIS FRIENDS?

AN "AYE!" PHONE, MATEY.

HOW DO SKELETONS FEEL AT THE END
OF A LONG DAY?

BONE TIRED.

WHAT DID THE VAMPIRE SAY TO BUFFY
AFTER SHE MADE HIM LAUGH?

"YOU SLAY ME!"

HAPPY HALLOWEEN!

# Silly Jokes

WHY DID THE CASHIER GET FIRED?

NOTHING SEEMED TO REGISTER WITH HIM.


WHAT'S THE HARDEST LIQUID TO CATCH?

RUNNING WATER.


WHAT DID THE LAMP SAY TO HIS WIFE?

"HONEY, YOU'RE ABSOLUTELY GLOWING!"


WHY DO SQUIRRELS TAKE SO MANY RISKS?

THEY'RE USED TO GOING OUT ON A LIMB.

WHY COULDN'T THE LEMON JUST
LET IT GO?

HE WAS STILL BITTER ABOUT IT.


WHY DID THE BIRD GET SO MAD
AT THE WIND?

IT REALLY RUFFLED HIS FEATHERS.


WHY CAN'T YOU JUDGE A BOOK
BY ITS COVER?

IT'S ALL A FRONT.


WHY DID THE OUTLET TAKE
COLD MEDICINE?

HE WAS ALL PLUGGED UP.

# How did the cell phone propose?

He gave her a ring.

# What does coffee say when it senses danger?

"There's trouble a-brewing!"

# What did the plate say after helping throw the birthday party?

"It was a piece of cake!"

# Why did the soldier have trust issues?

He was always on guard.

# WHO IS THE BEST PERSON TO SIT ON?

A CHAIRMAN.

# WHAT TYPE OF TREE IS PART OF YOUR HAND?

A PALM.

# WHAT KIND OF ART CAN YOU MAKE WITH YOUR TOES?

GRAFEETI.

# WHICH ANIMAL ALWAYS COPIES HIS FRIENDS' EXAMS?

A "CHEETAH."

# HOW DOES A HOAGIE GET TO WORK?

## THE SUBWAY.

# WHICH SUPERHERO ALWAYS HAS A QUESTION?

## WONDERING WOMAN.

# WHAT DO YOU CALL BREAD THAT'S AS HARD AS A STONE?

## ROCK N' ROLL

# WHY DID THE LOCOMOTIVE GO BACK TO SCHOOL?

## HE NEEDED TRAINING.

**WHY ARE TREES SAFER THAN DOGS?**

THEY'RE ALL BARK AND NO BITE.

**WHAT DID THE TREE SAY TO THE SKY AFTER BEING STRUCK BY LIGHTNING?**

"I'M SHOCKED!"

**WHY ARE TREES THE BEST CHEERLEADERS?**

THEY'LL ROOT FOR YOU.

**WHY DO NOODLES NOT LIKE BEING POURED OUT OF A POT?**

IT'S SUCH A STRAIN.

# WHY SHOULD YOU ASK A TREE FOR DIRECTIONS?

HE WILL GIVE YOU A GOOD ROUTE.

# WHY DID THE GYMNAST GO BANKRUPT?

SHE LOST HER BALANCE.

# WHY DO BELTS HAVE STAGE FRIGHT?

THEY BUCKLE UNDER PRESSURE.

# WHY DO TREES NOT MAKE VERY GOOD FRIENDS?

THEY LEAVE EVERY SPRING.

**WHAT DO YOU CALL A COW IN AN EARTHQUAKE?**

A MILKSHAKE.

**WHAT DID THE DOORKNOB SAY TO THE DOORSTOP?**

"I CAN HANDLE IT."

**WHY COULDN'T THE HUNGRY BOY GET HIS PEANUT BUTTER SANDWICH OUT OF THE BAG?**

IT WAS JAMMED.

**WHAT IS A TROPHY BEFORE IT'S UNWRAPPED?**

IT'S BOUND FOR GLORY.

WHAT DO YOU CALL A SHINY WOOD
TABLE THAT COMPLETES A RACE?

FINISH

WHY ARE RHINOCEROSES SO LOUD?

THEY HAVE BIG HORNS.

WHY DOES A GROCERY STORE NEVER
GET IN TROUBLE?

THEY'RE FULL OF GOODIES.

WHY WOULDN'T THE HORSE
STOP TALKING?

HE WAS STALLING.

WHY COULDN'T THE BROOM STAY AWAKE?

HE WAS SWEEPY.

WHY SHOULD YOU ALWAYS LISTEN
TO PENCILS?

BECAUSE THEY MAKE GOOD POINTS.

WHY ARE BASEBALL PLAYERS THE
BEST DANCERS?

BECAUSE THEY KEEP THEIR EYES ON THE BALL.

WHY ARE ROCKS SO PATIENT?

THEY HAVE A LOT OF WAIT.

WHY DID ALL THE CHILDREN PUT ON A
PERFORMANCE OF PETER PAN
IN THE PARK?

THEIR MOMS TOLD THEM TO GO OUTSIDE AND PLAY.


WHY ARE GOOD DOGS THE FASTEST DOGS?

THEY STAY IN THE LEAD.


WHY IS IT SO EASY TO CARRY
A LIGHT BULB?

IT'S VERY LIGHT.


WHY DOES IT TAKE SO LONG TO
PAINT A PICTURE?

YOU HAVE TO DRAW IT OUT.

WHY ARE PARADES BEST IN THE SPRING?

They're always on the March.

Two friends were warming up before gym class by touching their toes. One girl said, "Look! I can reach all the way to China!" The other girl replied, "Well that's a stretch!"

WHAT'S THE QUICKEST WAY FROM A TO Z?

You dash in between them.

WHAT DID RED SAY TO PURPLE?

"You've got a bad case of the blues."

Two astronauts were preparing for a trip to Mars. The first astronaut said, "Can I bring my extra luggage on the trip?" The second astronaut replied, "Sure. We've got plenty of space!"

Why did the grizzly hibernate all winter?

He couldn't bear the cold.

How many powerlifters does it take to change a lightbulb?

One. It's light.

How did one glass end it's relationship with the other?

They broke up.

WHAT ANIMAL IS BEST AT BASEBALL?

A BAT.

WHAT DID THE BOSS FLAME SAY
TO HIS WORKER?

YOU'RE FIRED.

WHAT DID THE MOTHER OWL SAY TO
HER FUNNY SON?

YOU'RE A HOOT.

WHERE DOES A TORNADO STOP
FOR LUNCH?

WENDY'S.

WHERE DOES A TREE KEEP ITS SPARE TIRE?

IN ITS TRUNK.


WHAT IS A GOLFER'S FAVORITE ANIMAL?

A BIRDIE.


WHY DID THE CELL PHONE GO TO JAIL?

IT WAS CHARGED.


WHAT DID THE SUN SAY TO THE
MOON AFTER ITS HOLLYWOOD DEBUT?

I'M A STAR.

WHAT DID THE KING OF HEARTS SAY
TO THE KING OF DIAMONDS WHEN
THEY AGREED ON SOMETHING?

YOU'VE GOT A DEAL.

WHY WAS THE COOKIE SO BROKEN?

IT WAS FULL OF CHOCOLATE CHIPS.

WHY DIDN'T THE POPSICLE GET
GOOD GRADES?

IT WAS TOO COOL FOR SCHOOL.

WHY DID THE WIND KEEP TRYING
TO IMPRESS PEOPLE?

IT WANTED TO BLOW THEIR MINDS.

**WHAT DID THE SHOVEL SAY TO THE DIRT?**

I'M REALLY DIGGING YOU.

**WHY DIDN'T THE COMPUTER TRUST THE MOBILE?**

IT WAS TOO PHONY.

**WHAT IS A POTATO'S FAVORITE DAY OF THE WEEK?**

FRIDAY

**WHAT DOES A WRITER USE TO MAKE THEIR BED?**

SHEETS OF PAPER.

**WHAT INSTRUMENT DOES A PIRATE PLAY WHEN HE WANTS PEOPLE TO GO AWAY?**

A-GETARRRRRRRRGH

**WHY WOULDN'T THE OWNER OF A CHINA SHOP LET CURIOUS GEORGE IN?**

SHE WANTED NO MONKEY BUSINESS.

**WHICH SHELLFISH THROWS BALLS THE BEST?**

A LOBSTER.

**WHAT DID ONE SAY TO TWO WHEN IT ASKED FOR HELP?**

YOU CAN COUNT ON ME.

WHY WAS THE WALL COLD?

IT NEEDED ANOTHER COAT.

WHAT'S A HOCKEY PLAYER'S
FAVORITE DESSERT?

CAKE. THEY LOVE iCiNG.

WHY WAS THE DAD UPSET ABOUT THE
HORSES ON STAGE?

HE HAD SAiD, "NO HORSEPLAY!"

WHY DiD YOGi TELL BOO BOO HE WOULDN'T
STEAL ANY MORE PiCNiC BASKETS?

HE COULDN'T BEAR TO EAT MORE.

Knock Knock. Who's there?
Shhh. Shhh, who?
Why would you want me to leave?
I just got here.


What was the wind's favorite color?

Blue


How come no one wanted to
talk to the pencil?

Because it liked to have long
drawn out conversations.


Why did the toilet paper go to Vegas?

It was on a roll.

WHAT SPORT DID THE SQUARE, CIRCLE, AND TRIANGLE TAKE UP?

FIGURE SKATING.

ONE MONKEY ASKED ANOTHER ONE, WHAT ARE YOU GOING TO DO TODAY? HE REPLIED, "NOT MUCH. JUST HANG AROUND."

WHAT LETTER IS SMALL, GREEN, AND GOOD FOR YOU?

P

WHY DID THE BOY IN LOVE HAVE SKINNED KNEES?

HE FELL HARD FOR A GIRL.

# WHAT KIND OF PLANT DO YOU NEED FOR BAKING?

Flour

# WHAT DOES ONE FLIRTATIOUS HAT SAY TO ANOTHER?

I FEDORYA.

# WHY DIDN'T THE FAN WIN THE RACE?

HE BLEW IT.

# WHY IS BREAD SO DEPENDABLE?

BECAUSE IT ALWAYS RISES TO THE OCCASION.

WHY DID THE SCISSORS MAKE THE TEAM?

THE MARKERS JUST COULDN'T CUT IT.


WHAT DID THE ROLLER COASTER SAY
WHEN THE AMUSEMENT PARK CLOSED?

"IT'S JUST NOT FAIR!"


WHY WAS THE FISH AFRAID TO WRITE
THE MOVIE REVIEW?

IT WAS ON A SCALE OF 1 TO 10.


HOW DID THE PAINTINGS GET OUT OF JAIL?

THEY FOUND OUT HE WAS FRAMED.

# WHY DIDN'T THE TOAST GO BACK TO COLLEGE?

HE WAS BURNT OUT.

# WHY WAS THE WHITE CRAYON SELF-CONSCIOUS?

BECAUSE HE PALED IN COMPARISON.

# WHY WAS THE CHEESE ALL TIED UP?

BECAUSE IT WAS STRING CHEESE.

# HOW DID THE DIAPER SAY HE WAS FEELING?

"JUST A LITTLE DOWN IN THE DUMPS."

# WHY CAN'T YOU TRUST PANTS?

THEY ALWAYS POCKET YOUR MONEY.


# WHAT DO YOU CALL SHOES THAT ARE UNDERCOVER?

SNEAKERS.


# HOW DO YOU KNOW TRAINS ARE BIG TATTLETALES?

THEY ALWAYS BLOW THE WHISTLE.


# WHAT HAPPENED WHEN THE WAVE GRADUATED FROM HIGH-SCHOOL?

HE SWELLED WITH PRIDE.

WHY DID THE CRAYON INSIST ON
WEARING A CROWN?

BECAUSE HE WAS ROYAL BLUE.


WHAT DOES THE HAMMER SAY AT THE
END OF THE WORKDAY?

"NAILED IT!"


WHY DO MOUNTAINS THINK THEY'RE
GOOD ROLE MODELS?

BECAUSE EVERYBODY LOOKS UP TO THEM.


HOW COULD THE FLUTE
REMEMBER EVERYTHING?

IT WAS ACTUALLY A RECORDER.

WHAT DID THE FOOT SAY TO HIS MOM
WHEN HE GOT IN A FIGHT AT SCHOOL?

"BUT MOM, HE SOCKED ME!"


WHICH COLOR IS ALWAYS GREETING PEOPLE?

YELLOW.


WHAT KIND OF SHOES DOES A
ROBBER WEAR?

SNEAKERS.


WHAT DID THE FOUR SLEEPY WHEELS
ON ONE CAR SAY TO THE FOUR WHEELS
ON ANOTHER CAR?

"WE'RE TIRED!"

WHAT DID ONE PLUMBER SAY TO THE WOMAN WHO WOULDN'T STOP SINGING?

"PIPE DOWN!"


WHAT COUNTRY NEVER DRINKS FROM A BOTTLE?

CANADA.


WHAT DID THE TEACHER BEE SAY TO THE STUDENT BEE?

"BEEHAVE!"


WHY DID THE LAMP NEED TO GAIN WEIGHT?

HE WAS A LITTLE LIGHT.

**WHAT DID THE DRIVER SAY AFTER MAKING A WRONG LEFT TURN?**

"That wasn't right..."

**HOW DID THE MOP AND BROOM ESCAPE THE COPS?**

They made a clean getaway.

**WHY WAS THE ELEVATOR KICKED OUT OF THE HAPPINESS CLUB?**

It kept bringing everyone down.

**WHY DID THE TWIG GET ATTACHED TO THE GROUND?**

It was a little stick-y.

WHAT'S A BALLOON'S LEAST FAVORITE
TYPE OF MUSIC?

POP.

WHAT COMPLIMENT DID THE COAT ON THE
RACK GIVE THE COAT ON THE FLOOR?

YOU'RE OFF THE HOOK.

HOW MUCH DOES A LIGHT BULB WEIGH?

A WATT.

WHAT DID THE PEN AND THE PENCIL
DO AT A DUEL?

DRAW THEIR WEAPONS.

Lightning Source UK Ltd.
Milton Keynes UK
UKHW020940070122
396769UK00010B/376